D1306676

EDGE BOOKS

PARANORMAL HANDBOOKS

HANDBOOK TO

GHOSTS, POLTERGEISTS, AND HAUNTED HOUSES

BY SEAN McCOLLUM

CAPSTONE PRESS
a capstone imprint

Edge Books are published by Capstone Press,
1710 Roe Crest Drive, North Mankato, Minnesota 56003.
www.mycapstone.com

Library of Congress Cataloging-in-Publication Data
Names: McCollum, Sean.
Title: Handbook to ghosts, poltergeists, and haunted houses / by Sean
  McCollum.
Description: North Mankato, Minnesota : An imprint of Capstone Press, [2017]
  | Series: Edge Books. Paranormal Handbooks | Includes bibliographical
  references and index. | Audience: Ages: 9–15. | Audience: Grades: 4 to 6.
Identifiers: LCCN 2016004343| ISBN 9781515713081 (Library Binding) | ISBN
  9781515713128 (eBook (PDF))
Subjects: LCSH: Ghosts—Juvenile literature. | Poltergeists—Juvenile
  literature. | Haunted places—Juvenile literature.
Classification: LCC BF1461 .M398 2017 | DDC 133.1—dc23
LC record available at http://lccn.loc.gov/2016004343

Editorial Credits
Nate LeBoutillier, editor; Philippa Jenkins, designer; Svetlana Zhurkin, media researcher;
Kathy McColley, production specialist

Photo Credits
Alamy: Classic Image, 6, Pictorial Press, 23, Wallace Weeks, 18; AP Photo: Mark Humphrey, 16;
Corbis: Bettmann, 20; Getty Images: The LIFE Picture Collection/David E. Scherman, 17; In-
ternational Mapping, 28 (middle); Library of Congress, 9, 21, 22; Newscom: Album/Laika En-
tertainment, 10, Danita Delimont Photography/Walter Bibikow, 28 (top middle), Design Pics,
11, Europics, 26, Mirrorpix, 12; Shutterstock: Africa Studio, 8, Anastasia Tveretinova, 14 (top),
Anki Hoglund, 27, Antlio, cover (bottom), 1, Arda Savasciogullari, 3, 29, Artistas, 14 (bottom),
Darla Hallmark, 28 (top left), Dmitry Zimin, 5, Everett Collection, 24, karenfoleyphotography,
28 (bottom right), katalinks, 7, KMcNamara, 28 (top right), Lario Tus, cover (top), back cover,
Mariusz S. Jurgielewicz, 28 (bottom left), nutech21, 25, Zack Frank, 28 (bottom middle)

Design Elements by Shutterstock

Printed and bound in China.
007721

TABLE OF CONTENTS

The Vanishing Hitchhiker

A couple of friends are driving on a dark road on a cold night. They are surprised to see a shivering teen girl. She is barefoot and not wearing a coat. They quickly pull over and pick her up.

The girl gets in the back seat and gives them the address where she lives. "My mother will be so worried," the girl says. They drive to an old house and pull into the driveway. The driver glances in the rearview mirror and gasps. Both friends turn around. The backseat is empty. The girl has mysteriously disappeared!

Mystified, the friends go to the door and are met by an old woman. They explain what happened and describe the girl they had picked up. "That sounds like my daughter," the old woman says. "She was killed in a car accident 20 years ago, near where you picked her up."

This ghost story is known as "The Vanishing Hitchhiker." Versions of it are told in many countries, including Korea, Japan, and the United States. Some people will swear it's true, saying they know the friends it happened to.

Few kinds of tales fascinate people like ghost stories. They exist in every culture. But do ghosts truly walk the Earth? Do they hitchhike its roads? Science has not found any proof that spirits of the dead exist. But that does not mean they do not haunt our imaginations.

CHAPTER 1

THE MYSTERY OF GHOSTS

One of the oldest ghost stories we know of appears in *The Epic of Gilgamesh*. This ancient poem is more than 4,200 years old. In it Gilgamesh and his fellow warrior Enkidu perform many heroic acts together. But after

Gilgamesh (right) helps Enkidu (left) best the Bull of Ishtar.

Enkidu dies, Gilgamesh seeks out his ghost in the underworld. With the help of two gods, the two friends are able to meet again.

The idea of ghosts is as old as human history. In most ghost stories, ghosts are spirits of dead people that appear to the living. At the heart of these tales is a very deep question: What happens to people when they die? Where do their feelings, memories, and personalities go? Science offers few answers to these questions. Therefore many people turn to religion and myth to explore them.

FREAKY FACT

A 2013 poll found that 42 percent of Americans believe that ghosts exist and 23 percent claim to have seen one.

Ghosts appear in many forms in legends and tales. Some ghosts are nasty and monstrous. Some "lost souls" are described as lonely and sad. Others are kind and helpful—or perhaps full of **mischief**. In many instances ghosts in these stories have unfinished tasks they want to finish. They may be inspired by true love, a wish to help others, or hunger for revenge.

mischief—playful behavior causing harm or trouble

Historical Ghosts

Reports of ghosts are often linked to historical events. Some spirits are said to be so heartbroken that they cannot leave the place where they died.

Queen Esther

In the mid-1700s, a battle took place in Pennsylvania. It pitted a group of white soldiers against an Iroquois village. According to some sources, the Indian warriors had been responsible for the killing of some white settlers. After a fierce fight, the soldiers overran the Iroquois village. Queen Esther, a young Iroquois leader, tried to get her people to safety. They were caught. According to one story, the soldiers forced Queen Esther to watch them drown all the women and children of her village. Then they **lynched** her.

Years after the massacre, settlers reported hearing screams in the forest. Hunters in the area have also told of seeing a weeping woman hanging from a tree branch—then she suddenly disappears.

lynch—to be murdered, often by hanging, by a mob

Ghosts of Gettysburg

In July 1863 a bloody battle of the U.S. Civil War (1861–1865) took place near Gettysburg, Pennsylvania. Thousands of soldiers were killed or wounded there. Since then some visitors to the battleground have reported hearing shouts, screams, and booms of distant cannons.

One hundred years after the war, two workers claimed to have seen ghostly wounded soldiers being cared for in a building basement. The building had been a hospital during the battle.

Battle of Gettysburg

Famous Ghosts in Stories and Movies

Writers and filmmakers have shared thousands of stories about ghosts. These portrayals contribute a lot to our ideas about ghosts and other spirits.

ParaNorman was nominated for a Best Animated Feature Academy Award.

FRIENDLY AND FUNNY GHOSTS	
Ghostbusters (1984, 2016)	A team of scientists uses its wits to save New York City from a spirit invasion.
ParaNorman (2012)	An 11-year-old boy uses his ability to speak with the dead to save his town and right a past wrong.
Beetlejuice (1988)	Two married ghosts call up a wild and crazy spirit named Beetlejuice. He helps save them and their haunted home.

FREAKY FACT

In the past, corpses were often wrapped in shrouds of white cloth before burial. This helps explain drawings of ghosts that look like they are wearing a bed sheet.

William Shakespeare's *Hamlet* featured Hamlet's father (right) in ghost form.

VENGEFUL AND FRIGHTFUL CHOSTS

Hamlet by William Shakespeare (about 1600)	Hamlet's father may be the most famous ghost in literature. Early in the play, the ghost of the former king tells his son that he had been murdered. Hamlet then sets out to **avenge** his father's death.
A Christmas Carol by Charles Dickens (1843)	In this famous book, Ebenezer Scrooge starts out as a mean, lonely man. But a visit from the chain-rattling ghost of his former business partner helps scare Scrooge into changing his ways.
Monster House (2006)	A team of kids discovers the secret of an evil house and works together to free spirits trapped there.

CHAPTER 2

POLTERGEISTS: TROUBLEMAKING SPIRITS

In 2006 a family in a small English town told of spooky goings-on in their home. Stuffed animals flew by themselves, hitting them in the head. Something seemed determined to yank the covers off the bed while they slept. Threatening messages showed up on their 3-year-old son's toys.

Poltergeists or Stressed Kids?

Some psychologists offer non-paranormal explanations for poltergeists. They note the activity often centers around one person in the home. Usually it is a child who is feeling especially unhappy or stressed. The child may be acting out his or her unhappiness by secretly causing trouble and doing damage. These children may have no memory of what they have done.

The family and **paranormal** researchers blamed the experience on a poltergeist. *Poltergeist* is a German term that means "noisy spirit." Unlike ghosts in ghost stories, poltergeists do not appear in visible form. Some ghost experts do not consider them ghosts at all.

Poltergeists are mainly mischief-makers. They are said to **inhabit** homes where they knock knick-knacks off shelves, throw objects, and toy with electronics. In extreme cases they have been accused of physically attacking victims.

Like ghosts, poltergeist activity has never been confirmed as a **supernatural** event. But stories about poltergeists often show up on the Internet. Some people even share online videos that supposedly show a poltergeists behaving badly.

paranormal—having to do with an event with no scientific explanation
inhabit—to live in
supernatural—something that cannot be given ordinary explanation

Five Levels of Poltergeist Activity

Paranormal researchers investigate reports of ghosts and poltergeists. Some claim poltergeists watch people in a house to figure out what scares them most.

The spirit's activity is said to grow more intense and dangerous as time passes. Researchers have divided the activity into five levels.

LEVEL 1
Getting Noticed

Pets may act up. People may hear odd noises, smell strange odors, feel unexplained cold spots in the house. They may sense that they are being watched.

LEVEL 2
Leaving Physical Signs

People may hear moaning. They may also feel breezes circulating in closed rooms.

LEVEL 3
Acting Annoying

Lights and electronics may turn on or off by themselves. People may feel like they are being touched or pushed.

LEVEL 4
Moving and Smashing

Furniture moves or shakes for no reason. Dishes and other objects are smashed. Loud voices come from nowhere.

LEVEL 5
Attacking

Victims are scratched, bitten, or slapped by unseen forces. They may be struck by flying objects. The poltergeist is sometimes accused of leaving threatening notes.

Famous Poltergeist Cases

The Bell Witch

The legend of the Bell Witch took place in Adams, Tennessee, from 1817-1821. According to accounts, the spirit pounded on walls of the Bell family home. It threw objects, spoke out loud, shook hands, and pinched and slapped people. Though the being was described as a "witch," it behaved like a poltergeist.

Carney Bell, a descendent of John Bell, posed for a 2003 photograph.

The "Danny" Poltergeist Case

In the 1990s an alleged poltergeist event occurred in Savannah, Georgia. The Cobb family bought an antique bed for their 14-year-old son, Jason. The bed seemed to come with a poltergeist, they later told investigators. An unseen force began moving and tossing objects, flipping chairs, and leaving notes. One note told who the spirit was: "Danny, 7." Another note explained that Danny's mother had died in the bed in 1899.

The Borley Rectory Poltergeist Hoax

In the 1930s Borley Rectory was considered the most haunted place in England. There were many reported incidents of unexplained activity there. These included the mysterious ringing of servant bells and a "magic" self-playing piano. Famous writers and investigators visited. They went away convinced a poltergeist was at work.

Years later, children who had lived in the house confessed it was all a hoax. They described how they rigged the bells, the piano, and other parts of the house to trick visitors into thinking it was haunted. Some people, however, are still convinced that it was a poltergeist's mischief.

The Borley Rectory was damaged by fire in 1939 (shown above) and demolished in 1944.

CHAPTER 3

HAUNTED PLACES: DON'T GO IN THERE!

New Orleans is famous for jazz, big parties, and fantastic food. But it has also been called the most haunted city in America.

the Andrew Jackson Hotel in New Orleans, Louisiana

Many sites there are said to be haunted. One is the Andrew Jackson Hotel. It was built on the site of an all-boys boarding school that burned down in 1788. Stories say five boys died in the flames.

More recently some hotel guests have complained that toilets flush for no reason and TVs change channels by themselves. Then there are the noisy kids playing in the courtyard—noisy kids who are not seen.

Old hotels and houses are ripe for ghost reports. Visitors may report strange voices, odd smells, slamming doors, and other unexplained phenomena. Creaky stairs, antique furniture, dark corners, and old-fashioned portraits of people long since dead can all contribute to the eeriness.

Reports about haunted places often tell of some awful event that happened there long ago. Misery and murder are common themes. Ghostly victims are often described as being trapped in a place by heartbreak. Other spirits are said to be unaware they are dead.

FREAKY FACT

Many cities and towns feature "ghost tours." Guides share the history of the area and take tourists to sites rumored to be haunted.

Infamous Haunted Houses in America

Wherever you live, someplace nearby is likely said to be haunted. It might be a cemetery. It might be an old farmhouse. It might even be the home of the president of the United States.

The House in Amityville

Amityville is a quiet village on Long Island, New York. But in 1974 a horrible crime happened in a house there. A man shot and killed six members of his family.

A year later, another family moved into that same house. Family members reported experiencing a series of very scary events. The mother was lifted off her bed and left floating in the air. They said they saw visions of creatures,

the house in Amityville

including a demon-like pig. Green slime oozed from walls and the keyhole in the kids' playroom. The family moved out after only 28 days. Their story is retold in the book *The Amityville Horror*.

White House Hauntings?

The White House has stood for more than 200 years. It is easy to imagine famous people walking its historic hallways. The ghosts of several are said to still haunt the house, including Abraham Lincoln. Visitors also tell of seeing Abigail Adams, the wife of President John Adams, hanging laundry.

Abraham Lincoln

Myrtles Plantation

Myrtles Plantation in Louisiana has been called the most haunted house in America. Several murders took place there in the past. One man was shot and died on the main staircase of the house. Today the place is a bed and breakfast hotel. Guests and employees say they have heard the ghost of the dying man crawling up the stairs. Other ghostly experiences are commonly reported as well.

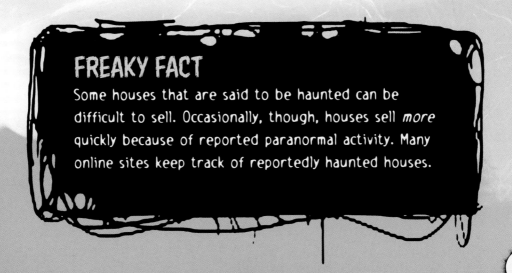

FREAKY FACT

Some houses that are said to be haunted can be difficult to sell. Occasionally, though, houses sell *more* quickly because of reported paranormal activity. Many online sites keep track of reportedly haunted houses.

Other Haunted Places

Haunted houses are not the only places ghosts supposedly hang out. Ghostly reports are also common in ships, theaters, and abandoned buildings.

The USS *Constellation*

The USS *Constellation* was one of the first warships ever built for the U.S. Navy. It was launched in 1797 and saw action in several wars. Today the restored ship is a floating museum in Baltimore, Maryland. One reported spirit is that of Thomas Truxton, the USS *Constellation's* first captain. An account says that his ghost even guided unsuspecting visitors on a tour of his old ship.

The USS *Constellation.*

Theatre Royal of Drury Lane

Almost every playhouse has a ghost story. The Theatre Royal in London, England, has been around since the 1600s. It is reportedly haunted by the "Man in Grey." He is described as a gentleman dressed in clothing from the 1700s. Witnesses sometimes report him wandering among

Joseph Grimaldi

the seats. Another ghost there is said to be of the famous clown Joseph Grimaldi. Some anxious actors describe feeling his calming spirit while onstage.

Willard Asylum for the Chronically Insane

Asylums are notorious for being haunted. Willard Asylum for the Chronically Insane in Ovid, New York, was abandoned long ago. But visitors have reported seeing a ghostly red-headed patient there. She has been reported walking the hallways, letting out occasional midnight screams.

asylum—hospital for people who are mentally ill

CHAPTER 4

PURSUING THE PARANORMAL

What would you want to know if you could converse with the dead? The question fascinates many who are interested in ghosts and spirits.

Séances and Mediums

Curiosity about the afterlife leads some people to take part in **séances**. These meetings were especially popular in the 1800s. **Mediums** might go into a trance and then answer questions people had for dead relatives. Sometimes the ritual

séance—meeting to contact spirits of the dead
medium—a person who claims to make contact with spirits of the dead

included mysterious events, like floating tables or "spirit slates" on which supposed messages from the dead appeared.

The Fox sisters gained fame as mediums in the 1850s. Young Kate and Margaret asked questions. A spirit would supposedly answer "yes" or "no" by the number of knocks.

In 1888 Kate and Margaret confessed they had completely faked their act. But by then their demonstrations had sparked a new religion called Spiritualism. Spiritualists believe that the living can communicate with the dead.

The popularity of séances eventually caught the attention of **skeptics**. In the 1880s a commission from the University of Pennsylvania launched an investigation. Every medium was found to be a fake. They used stage tricks to fool audiences and customers. Even so, mediums and psychics continue to make a living today by appealing to people hoping to contact the dead.

FREAKY FACT

Ouija boards first appeared in 1891 and are still popular today. Some people consider this "game" a way to communicate with ghosts and spirits.

skeptic—a person doubtful of paranormal events

A modern ghost hunter checks his equipment.

Ghost Hunting Today

The hobby of ghost hunting continues to grow. Several reality TV shows about exploring haunted places have become popular.

Today's ghost hunters make a show of using high-tech gear. This electronic equipment often includes:

- handheld meters that can detect changes in electromagnetic fields
- photographic and video cameras that use lenses that can see in the dark
- infrared thermometers that can measure changes in room temperature
- digital recorders to capture mysterious noises and sounds

These devices look very professional. Ghost hunters claim they can pinpoint paranormal activity. However, there is no evidence this is the case.

Almost all trained scientists consider paranormal investigation a **pseudoscience**. Chemistry, biology, physics, and other scientific fields use experiments to prove or disprove an idea. Ghost hunting cannot do the same.

Without proof why are we still so fascinated by ghosts? Perhaps we are very curious about what happens to people when they die. We want to know if the human spirit lives on after the heart beats for the last time. For that reason we will never stop exploring ghost stories—and trying to prove ghosts' existence.

pseudoscience—a field of study that makes claims that cannot be proven

Haunted Hot Spots in the U.S.

Here are eight famous haunted sites in the United States.

They are worthy of more research—or in-person exploring.

VILLISCA AXE MURDER HOUSE,
Villisca, Iowa

THE STANLEY HOTEL,
Estes Park, Colorado

THE LINCOLN THEATER,
Decatur, Illinois

THE OHIO STATE REFORMATORY,
Mansfield, Ohio

EASTERN STATE PENITENTIARY,
Philadelphia, Pennsylvania

MISSION SAN MIGUEL,
San Luis Obispo, California

ST. LOUIS CEMETERY,
New Orleans, Louisiana

TRANS-ALLEGHENY LUNATIC ASYLUM,
West Viriginia

HANDBOOK QUIZ

1. What contributes a lot to our ideas about ghosts and other spirits?

a. scientific research
b. stories and movies
c. historical reports
d. personal experience

2. How are poltergeists different from ghosts?

a. Ghosts are more dangerous than poltergeists.
b. Ghosts are noisier than poltergeists.
c. Poltergeists don't appear in visible form, but ghosts do.
d. Poltergeists are not real but ghosts are.

3. What do places that are reportedly haunted often have in common?

a. They have a history of violence, murder, or misery.
b. They are very old.
c. They have been abandoned and are now empty.
d. Dead bodies have been found there.

4. What do séances and mediums try to do?

a. find scientific proof of ghosts and other spirits
b. communicate with spirits of the dead
c. join the religion of Spiritualism
d. entertain people with stage magic

5. Why do most scientists consider ghost hunting a pseudoscience?

a. Ghost hunters are well-trained.
b. Anyone can claim to be a ghost hunter.
c. Ghost hunters have high-tech gear, like real scientists.
d. It is impossible for ghost hunters to prove ghosts exist.

Answers: 1-b, 2-c, 3-a, 4-b, 5-d

GLOSSARY

asylum (uh-SY-luhm)—hospital for people who are mentally ill

inhabit (in-HAB-it)—to live in

lynch (LINCH)—to be killed, often by hanging, by a mob

medium (MEE-dee-uhm)—a person who claims to make contact with spirits of the dead

mischief (MIS-chif)—playful behavior causing harm or trouble

paranormal (par-uh-NORE-muhl)—having to do with an event that has no scientific explanation

pseudoscience (SU-doh-sy-ens)—a field of study that makes unproveable claims

séance (SAY-ahns)—meeting to contact the spirits of the dead

skeptic (SKEP-tik)—a person who questions things that other people believe in

supernatural (soo-pur-NACH-ur-uhl)—something that cannot be given ordinary explanation

READ MORE

Raij, Emily. *Ghosts of the Rich and Famous.* Spooked. North Mankato, Minn.: Capstone Press, 2016.

Raij, Emily. *The Most Haunted Places in the World.* Spooked. North Mankato, Minn.: Capstone Press, 2016.

INTERNET SITES

FactHound offers a safe, fun way to find Internet sites related to this book. All of the sites on FactHound have been researched by our staff.

Here's all you do:

Visit *www.facthound.com*

Type in this code: 9781515713081

Check out projects, games and lots more at
www.capstonekids.com

INDEX